Anonymous

Christian Heroism in Death

Christian heroism in death the experience of Jasper Stickland, of Milborne

Port - the experience of Jasper Stickland, of Milborne Port

.

Anonymous

Christian Heroism in Death
Christian heroism in death the experience of Jasper Stickland, of Milborne Port - the experience of Jasper Stickland, of Milborne Port

ISBN/EAN: 9783337194956

Printed in Europe, USA, Canada, Australia, Japan

Cover: Foto © Lupo / pixelio.de

More available books at **www.hansebooks.com**

CHRISTIAN HEROISM IN DEATH.

THE EXPERIENCE OF

JASPER STICKLAND,

OF MILBORNE PORT,

WHO ENTERED INTO REST, JUNE 5TH, 1867,

AGED 34 YEARS.

"If so be that we suffer with Him, that we may be also glorified together."—Rom. viii. 17.

LONDON:

PRINTED FOR PRIVATE CIRCULATION.

1867.

LONDON
PRINTED BY HAYMAN BROTHERS & CO.,
GOUGH SQUARE, E.C.

PREFACE.

THE subject of the following pages was a Wesleyan-Methodist, and was employed as a leather-parer in the glove trade, the prevailing industry of this place.

I need not detail the circumstances which appeared to cast upon me the duty of delivering an address on the occasion of his death. I will only say, it was undesigned and unexpected. To persons in this neighbourhood I need not speak of myself; but some into whose hands this little tract may fall, may wish to know who and what I am, and why I present myself to the public. For the satisfaction of such persons, I would say, I am a glove manufacturer, and employ a large number of persons in the locality. I am also a Wesleyan-Methodist, and what is termed a "Local Preacher" in that body. I come before the world on this occasion, I humbly trust, because the love of Christ constrains me, and for two reasons.

First, I see society around me needs the religion implied in the above principle, and so beautifully illustrated in the case of this poor glover. I need not say how religion dignifies labour, and elevates, refines, and purifies every one that is brought under its influence ; how it adds lustre to the coronet and the crown ; and how it ennobles persons of low degree. But for religion to work such wonders, it must not be a dead thing, a mere formal thing, anything hereditary, sentimental, or matter of opinion. It is the vitality of the Word of God, and the simplicity and power of the Gospel of Christ, that I designate religion ; and though I do not wish we may have less of the *form* of religion* amongst us than we have at present, I would that we possessed much more of its power. And I would observe,

* Certain eccentric observances prevalent in some quarters now a-days can scarcely be called the form of RELIGION : let us not turn away from the *form*, but from these caricatures—alas !

however the form of godliness may abound, if it be destitute of the power, it is nothing worth. A living Christianity is the want of the age, and nothing short of this will suffice.

My second reason is, I want provision to be made for the widow and fatherless children of this good man. I would not leave them to depend on parish pay. This is a merciful provision for many; and I hope the time will come when our poor-law system will be improved and made less obnoxious to many of the deserving poor; for I hail with joy and hope the improvement which has been lately made in its administration in London.

Jasper Stickland was a provident man, and a member of the society of Foresters, by whom, in the lodge to which he belonged, as with all others who ever knew him, he was highly esteemed. Had he lived a few months longer, his widow and children, at his death, would have been entitled to some five shillings per week; but now, for want of the completed period, this is lost to them. However, there is, I am informed,

in that deserving Institution, a custom of
making a collection at the several lodges for
the benefit of such cases as the present; and
as this is a perfectly voluntary offering, more
or less is given according to what is known
of the case for which the appeal is made.
It is intended to send a copy of this publi-
cation to the lodges of this society, the members of which will only be too happy to
subscribe towards so deserving and so
necessitous a case. Then it is believed that
many who read this brief memoir will feel
a sympathy with its subject, whose hearts
have been kindled by the same altar-fire.
To many such, the appeal will not be made in
vain. There are others who, from causes I
need not specify, have but little sympathy
for religion of that active and stirring character here presented to view, but who can
appreciate the honest and struggling efforts
of the deserving poor, and who have a tear
to drop upon their sorrows, and a dole to
give towards their wants. To benevolent
persons of this description, to honest and
upright minds, this appeal will not be in vain.

Of the widow and nine fatherless children, the youngest in arms and the eldest under fifteen years of age, I may say, that they are worthy : of the elder ones, more industrious, better conducted, and more hopeful children I have not seen.

In the expectation of Christians and kind-hearted people assisting in this truly charit-able undertaking, I take on myself the responsibility of supporting this family, with-out parish aid, and bringing them up in the circumstances to be expected had their father lived. There is no intention to lift them out of their own proper sphere ; this would be doing them no service. And if ever they rise in society, as some of them already promise to do, it will not be by any *patronage*, but by their own honest endeav-ours and God's good blessing.

I was in a distant part of the country on the day of interment. The funeral was deeply affecting. A short account will be found at the close (Appendix B), kindly sup-plied by the respected Superintendent of the Circuit, the Rev. E. Fison.

I will only further add, that the following discourse was taken down in short-hand, at my own request, by the able reporter of the "Sherborne Journal," and is presented to you with only those few verbal corrections which an extemporaneous address required. It is of the discourse that I here speak; the memoir of the sick and dying chamber embodied in it, was read from manuscript, and is presented as it was delivered at the Wesleyan Chapel, Milborne Port, to a large and attentive congregation, on the Sunday evening of June 16th.*

THOMAS ENSOR.

Milborne Port,
     June 25, 1867.

* To Mr. Perks I am deeply indebted for examining the manuscript and passing these sheets through the press.

REFERENCES are kindly permitted to—

- SIR W C. MEDLYCOTT, Bart., Ven House, Milborne Port.
- The Rev. C. M. DE P. GILLAM, Vicar of Milborne Port.
- THE REV. W. ARTHUR, M.A., President of the Wesleyan Conference, Glendun, East Acton, Middlesex.
- SIR FRANCIS LYCETT, Sheriff of London and Middlesex, 18, Highbury Grove, London.
- WILLIAM M'ARTHUR, Esq., Sheriff of London and Middlesex elect, 1, Gwydyr Villas, Brixton, London.
- The Rev. GEORGE T. PERKS, M.A., 17, Alwyne Road, Canonbury, London.
- CHARLES CROKAT, Esq., 106, Fenchurch Street, London.

By any of these gentlemen, as well as by myself, subscriptions will be received and duly acknowledged. Should the contributions exceed what is required, the surplus will be applied to kindred objects, or for the furtherance of the Gospel, as a Committee who will have the management of the fund may direct.

———∘∘⦂⚫⦂∘∘———

CHRISTIAN HEROISM
IN DEATH.

"If so be that we suffer with Him, that we may be also glorified together."—Rom. viii. 17.

I WOULD first introduce you to the Master this evening, and then to the disciple— that disciple, doubtless, whom Jesus loved, and has just taken to Himself. When Andrew had found the Saviour, he first met with his brother Simon, and brought him at once to Jesus. On a festival occasion at Jerusalem certain Greeks came to Philip, and said, "Sir, we would see Jesus." They had come up from a distance,—from a far country, to see the Lord; and when they were in the place where Jesus was likely to be found, they met with some of His follow- ers,—some that loved Him,—some that could tell them where He was, the Master, the

Saviour; and they said (rightly, properly, and graciously moved by the Spirit of God), "Sir, we would see Jesus." Well, then, I would first direct your attention to Jesus; and I hope that all present this evening have the desire of those Greeks, and that you have come here to God's house, on this solemn occasion, to see Jesus; and if this be so, then I will promise you in my Master's name that He will see you, and that He will reveal Himself unto you. The text speaks of suffering and glory. We shall take these in their natural order: First we shall speak of the suffering, and then of the glory; after we have spoken of the suffering and glory referred to, I shall endeavour to present to your view the disciple.

First of all, we are to show you Christ, and then the reflected image of Christ; and I wish you all to compare the portrait with the glorious original, and I promise you shall see the likeness. The disciple bore the very lineaments and graces of the Master, for he had learnt of Him.

"If so be that we suffer with Christ, that

we may be also glorified together." Suffering seems to be the lot of humanity It is
said, "We come into the world with a cry, and
we depart out of the world with a groan."
This world is a vale of tears; man is born
to trouble as the sparks fly upwards; therefore, suffering is no stranger in this world.
You have not to travel far to find him out;
alas! we are all too well acquainted with
him ; he is far too familiar with us all. But
we cannot dwell on the amount of suffering,
and the great aggregation and complication
of suffering which we see in the world;
that mountain elevation, sometimes heaped
up together, and under which afflicted humanity groans. We need not point you to
the carnage of the battle-field ; we need not
take you to the horrors of the mad-house;
we need not dwell upon these things, because
you are too well acquainted with suffering;
and you all know, the youngest and the
most inexperienced of you, what it is to suffer.
But in our text, with regard to suffering,
there is this peculiarity: "If so be that we
suffer *with* Him" (that is with Christ). Our

blessed•Lord here occupies the foreground;
He is the most prominent object in all this
wide scene of suffering. We have read of
His sufferings and His death. Shall we
contemplate them? Now His sufferings
were for us; they were not endured on His
own account. Oh, no! We endure suffering
as the fruit and consequence of our sin: not
so Christ. He was holy, harmless, undefiled,
and higher than the heavens; there was no
spot, or blemish, or stain of sin about Him.
Then, why should Christ suffer? It was for
us: He suffered our punishment. There
was something penal in the sufferings
of Christ. They were not, so to speak,
natural sufferings; and, in some sense,
they were not necessary sufferings: they
were penal sufferings; they were inflicted by
law. He received weight and measure
according to law; and it was because the
law demanded it that Christ suffered. But
why? Because He stood in the place of the
guilty. Here was this world of ours exposed to all the wrath of God—a world left
to the undying worm and the consuming

fire; and our race was helples sand hopeless—withont strength; and there we stood, condemned and exposed to all the wrath and indignation of God. Could we atone for our transgressions? Would rivers of oil and seas of blood wash out the guilty stain? It was not possible that the blood of bulls and goats could take away sin. They · were offered np for thousands of years, and ceased not to be offered up: the offering that was made yesterday was repeated to-day, and will be repeated again to-morrow; and in every new offering there was the remembrance of sin; and man stood helpless. Then said Christ, "Lo! I come to put away sin by the sacrifice of Myself!" This was the reason and the cause of the Incarnation. It was necessary that He should partake of the nature of those that were to be redeemed; and He was thus made flesh, that in the flesh He might suffer for us; and it was on Calvary that He poured forth His heart's blood, and then, when He had made by that offering a full and complete satisfaction for the sins of all the world, He ex-

claimed, "It is finished," and gave up the
Ghost. This suffering was expiatory as
well as penal. Divine justice was satisfied;
the price was paid down for man; and now,
through the offering of Christ, every poor
sinner may claim his pardon, and go free.

But in the text we are said to suffer with
Him. "If so be that we suffer with Him."
Who are they that suffer with Christ? and in
what sense is it that they suffer with Christ?
"If *we* suffer with *Him;*"—surely it is not
everybody that suffers with Christ. In the
work of atonement he had no participator,
no companionship: there was no one to
share that work with our Lord. He was
alone; he trod the wine-press alone, and of
the people there was none with Him. Oh,
no! our sufferings will not add one iota to
the work of his cleansing and salvation. Oh,
no! Christ stood *alone* here; no man, no angel
suffered with Him in this sense. But there
must be a sense in which some people suffer
with Christ. Our text says, "If so be that
we suffer with Him." Now who is it that
suffers with Christ? Surely not all of us;

not everybody We hear Him exclaiming,
we hear Him complaining, " Is it nothing to
you, all ye that pass by, behold, see if there
be any sorrow like unto My sorrow which is
done unto Me, wherewith the Lord hath
afflicted Me in the day of His fierce anger ?"

May I ask you, my friends, who among
you have sympathized with your Lord ?
Who among you have mingled your tears
with His tears ? Who can say, in the language of the hymn,—

> " O Thou dear suffering Son of God,
>   How doth Thy heart to sinners move !
> Help me to catch Thy precious blood ;
>   Help me to taste Thy dying love.
>
> " Give me to feel Thine agonies ;
>   One drop of Thy sad cup afford :
> I fain with Thee would sympathize,
>   And share the sufferings of my Lord."

Yes, dear friends, there are those who
thus sympathize with Christ; there are those
who feel for Him, and are bound up in the
sufferings of Christ. There are those of this
congregation to whom this matter is no
strange thing, who can and do sympathize

with Christ, and share the sufferings of their Lord. Yes, all who love Christ sympathize with Him; all who believe in Christ value His sufferings in His atoning sacrifice; and they say,—for it is their language as truly as the Apostle's,—" God forbid that I should glory save in the cross of our Lord Jesus Christ." They cling to that cross; there they lose their burden; it is their light, and life, and joy.

> " None but Christ to me be given;
> None but Christ in earth or heaven."

I will not dwell further on the sufferings of Christ; they are portrayed to you in that prophetic Psalm (xxii.) read in the lesson for this evening, and which I entreat you to read when you retire from this place, in prayer to God, that you may feel what the Saviour endured for you.

Not only are the sufferings of Christ alluded to in the text, but our sufferings are likewise taken notice of. Contemplating those sufferings, infinite and unfathomable, how shall we speak of our own? We are reminded of

what David said to Saul, when he was pur-
suing him with relentless fury : "After
whom is the King of Israel come out?
After whom dost thou pursue? After a
dead dog? After a flea?" (1 Sam. xxiv. 14.)
That is, he was so thoroughly insignificant
that it was beneath the king's dignity
to come forth and fight against him ;
and surely, my friends, when we speak of
the sufferings of Christ, our own sufferings
seem altogether lost, and we can scarcely
bring them into account. Yet, for Heaven
to notice our sufferings at the same time
and associate them with the sufferings of our
Lord! and yet it is in the text, "If so be
that we suffer with Him." Well, then, believers suffer—not to dwell upon their sufferings—they have sufferings, in common with
other people, for religion was never designed
to exempt us from the common lot of
mortality; but they also have sufferings
which the world knows nothing of. Oh!
what pain and grief they experience at
times, that the stranger intermeddles not
with ; therefore their sufferings stand apart

from the sufferings of their fellows who have not yet believed in Christ.

But in reference to these sufferings, there are many alleviations. We would observe this. It is an alleviation to know that they suffer only in measure : the Lord does not lay upon His people more than He will enable them to bear ; and if they are called to suffer, their gracious Saviour is able to proportion the severity of the trial to the strength He gives to bear it. When the Apostle cried out under the pressure of his agonizing trial, when he besought the Lord that the affliction might depart from him, Jesus spoke gracious words of promise, hope, and comfort : " My grace is sufficient for thee." The trial continued ; but grace was given which made the Apostle superior to the trial, and enabled him to rejoice and glory in tribulation : " When I am weak, then am I strong." Thus, then, by trials and afflictions believers are corrected and sanctified. Look at the vine sending forth its luxuriant branches, spreading forth and growing upwards and all around. What a glorious plant ! But the wise and skilful gardener comes with his pruning hook, and lops here and there, and the plant to an inexperienced observer seems shorn and stripped of its glory, and appears a barren thing; but the vine-dresser knows what he is doing,— "Every branch that bringeth forth fruit, He purgeth it, that it might bring forth more fruit;" and then, when after an interval, we revisit the place and examine the vine, we see it laden with ripe and delicious fruit, instead of being covered with withered leaves. By afflictions and sufferings, then, God's people are corrected and sanctified.

But then observe further, that they suffer with Christ. Here it is permitted to believers to sympathize with their Master, to visit Bethlehem with Christ, Gethsemane and Calvary; and then, when He is taken down from the Cross and laid in the grave, they go there to weep. Well, then, and what about Christ? Is He as sympathizing as His disciples? What think you, as the disciples sympathize with the Master,

does the Master sympathize with the disciples? Why, in all their afflictions He is
afflicted. We have not a High Priest that
cannot be touched with the feeling of our
infirmities; He was in all points tempted
like as we are; and He knows how to sympathize, because He has Himself suffered.
How does this lighten the load! What
wonders the presence of Christ does for the
sufferer! How he rises above his pain! Oh,
how he blesses those sufferings which bring
to him the sympathy of his Lord! Yes,
Christ suffered, and suffers still, with His
people; not a suffering they endured is
unnoticed by Him; He is with them to
support them, He directs and regulates their
trials, and finally delivers them out of
them all; for He is made of God to His
people, not only wisdom, righteousness,
and sanctification, but He is made redemp-
tion also. There is not one enemy, or one
danger, or one difficulty, but He can deliver
deliver them; yea, He can save unto the
uttermost all who come unto God by Him.

We will pass on now to notice the glory

spoken of in the text: "If so be that we
suffer with Him, that we may be also glorified
together." We can dwell but briefly on this
part of our subject. It has been brought
before you in that sublime and transcendent
chapter of St. John (xvii.) which I just now
read ; and if I said none other word, surely
that is sufficient, yea, and more than sufficient; but we may notice, that though
the glory to be revealed is here spoken
of, yet there was a *measure* of glory which
Christ received in this world in His humili-
ation and suffering. Why there was a
glory about the birth of Christ ; and there
was glory at His baptism ; and there was
glory in that voice from heaven which said,
"This is my beloved Son, in whom I am well
pleased ;" when the Spirit of God descended
and alighted upon Him like a dove ; and then,
on the mount of transfiguration there was a
glory shining about the Lord, and reflecting
itself upon the three Apostles who were
associated with Him on the mount. But
these were only intimations, earnests, and
foretastes of that fulness of glory which He

was anticipating, when He was to receive glory, and dominion, and power of the Father, and to sit down on His right-hand; but here upon earth, the scene of conflict and toil, Christ was cheered by the glorious prospect that was set before Him whilst He endured the cross and despised the shame. And this glory, this future glory, was the subject of the ardent prayers of Christ when He was upon earth. Now let us see how this corresponds with experience; "we shall be glorified together." To those who are one with Christ, in perfect sympathy and perfect accord, Christ's cross is their cross; therefore Christ's glory is their glory: as Christ had the earnest of glory, so believers have the earnest of glory; as Christ had Heaven dwelling in His heart when on earth, so believers have heaven brought down to their souls whilst tabernacling in the flesh; and whatever belongs to Christ belongs to them. If Christ is seated on the throne, they are to be seated by His side on the same throne: "For it became Him for whom are all things and by whom are all things,

in bringing many sons unto glory, to make
the Captain of their salvation perfect through
suffering ;"—" For our light affliction, which
is but for a moment, worketh for us a far
more exceeding and eternal weight of
glory."

Having thus exhibited the Master, I have
now to place before you the servant, and
show the likeness he bore to his Divine Master. Jesus having loved His own who were
in the world, loved them to the end. What
would our late beloved brother say, if, from
the spirit-land, he could speak to us? His
last word on earth was " Christ ;" could he
return, his first word would be " Christ." It
may be truly said, from the first day of his conversion to the day of his death he preached
Christ. Christ was magnified in all the
relations and circumstances of life,—in his
sorrows and in his joys, in health and in sick-
ness, in life and in death. Whether in the
church or in the world, in active duty or in
passive suffering, he honoured and glorified
his Saviour, and effectually and powerfully
preached Christ. From the margin of his

grave, I would repreach this sermon, by telling you what he was, and what grace did for him. I would seek to honour the Saviour whom he so much loved, and to whom, could he revisit us, with all the ardour of his beatified spirit, he would point every poor sinner. My design is not to eulogize the dead; it is the living Jesus I would exalt; and if I mention the excellencies of our departed brother, it is only that God might be glorified in him.

I will not dwell on his state as a sinner; suffice it that I say, that he felt it to be such that he needed conversion and salvation. Before his conversion there was a dawning of good in him. He was a teacher in the Church Sunday-school. He was also accustomed to read good and instructive books: not the vile trash, the diluted elixir of hell,—I do not refer to standard works of taste and genius, but to the sensational and demoralizing novels of the day, so pernicious to youth, and so scandalous to persons of riper years,—but good wholesome literature, which led, if not to God, at least to

good. There was no doubt, as there often
is, a preparatory work; but the proximate
cause of conversion was a revival service at
Sherborne, eleven years ago, to which he
was invited and taken by his brother, who
some years before was called into the fellowship of the Gospel, and made a partaker of
the grace of Christ. Depend on it the converted will convert others. God said to
Abraham, I will bless thee, and make thee a
blessing. At this meeting a soldier prayed—
a good soldier of Queen Victoria, but one
faithful to King Jesus as well. In his prayer,
probably led by his own calling, he referred
to the soldier who thrust the spear into our
Saviour's side, and exclaimed, "Glory be to
God, here's one that is washed in the fountain." Jasper was close to the soldier, and
felt struck through as with a dart. It
was an arrow from the Almighty, and the
Spirit quickened his soul. In that moment,
like Paul on the way to Damascus, he
yielded to Christ, and in the same meeting
found peace. This was the day of decision;
with Joshua he said, "As for me and my

house, we will serve the Lord." He at once commenced family prayer. Not having confidence to offer extemporary prayer, he used a form ; but, in about a fortnight, the liberty of soul he felt induced him to throw away the crutches, as he said, and for ever after he realized both the gift and grace of prayer. And how he prayed, many who now hear me are witnesses. How humble, how fervent, how believing. There was boldness without irreverence, confidence without presumption, strong feeling without extravagance. Deep self-abasement tempered lively joy, and kept the mind nicely balanced, as it became a weak and sinful creature in the presence of the Infinite and the Holy. How many here will recognise his earnest pleading and simple approach to God :—

> " Just as I am,—without one plea
> But that Thy blood was shed for me,
> And that Thou bidd'st me come to Thee,—
> O Lamb of God, I come.

Having found peace, and reared an altar to God in his house, he extended his charity

to those around him. He became a Prayer-
Leader, Distributor of Tracts, took charge of
a Bible-class in the Sunday School, occasionally preached in the villages, and was
appointed a Class-Leader. His health pre-
vented his continuing to preach; but during
the brief period and the few occasions of his
exercising in this way the Lord gave him
fruit, and there are now members of our
church who were converted under God
through him. In all the other departments
of Christ's service he continued to the end,
abounding more and more, to the great edifi-
cation and delight of those who were
privileged with his services.

As a Class-Leader he had peculiar qualifi-
cations. His own experience was clear.
His was no doubtful profession. He
walked with God; and, like the good man,
out of the good treasure of his heart he
brought forth good things, for the encouragement, comfort, and instruction of those
committed to his care. Ho carefully
watched over his members, faithfully lead
them on, and was always at his post. Those

who met with him very highly prized him, and now deeply mourn his loss. He spoke words of encouragement to the feeble, like the good Shepherd who carried the lambs in His bosom, and gently led those who were with young. " Cheer on the members," he would say : " Poor, timid ones, try again." He mourned over the fallen. Let such as once met with him, and now feel the back-sliders' misery, think of his instructions, his warnings, his prayers. Let them hear his dying admonition. He said to one, " You'll need religion when you come here : it is enough to do *with* Christ, but the Lord have mercy upon that man who has to do without Christ."

Here let me remark on one feature of religion which peculiarly distinguished him, and which is suggested by the remark " Cheer on the members." His was a joyous religion. This made him strong, active, hopeful, and glad. The joy of the Lord was his strength. He loved his Master, and served Him with a glad heart and free. He did **not** loiter or lumber along ; **there** was no mopishness or despondency; but he went on his way blithely, and merrily, and agilely. His beaming countenance was good to look upon, and he diffused his own cheerful happy spirit all around. To be right there must be joy. I admit there's a time to weep, as well as a time to laugh; but I say, without hesitation, that religion is libelled by a gloomy countenance; and if any people under the sky have a right to be merry and happy, it is the people of God. With Christ in them, and the hope of glory, can it be otherwise?

About six years ago Jasper had a very severe illness, and was brought very low It seemed to him and to many that his departure was at hand, and he was *ready*. But it pleased the Lord to raise him up again, probably in answer to prayer, and for further usefulness. But for his cheerful acquiescence in the will of God, he would rather have complained of this; he was just putting into port, and it seemed hard to put back to sea again. Thus the prize at that time escaped his grasp, and he felt a degree of disappointment. But he learnt to wait; he knew, though the Lord delayed His coming, that He would come and not tarry. But this interval of years was a blessed season to himself and his family, the Church, and the world; for all have benefited by his life and example.

But now the time came for our friend to die. It was hard to give him up. There were reasons, strong reasons, why he should live, were it the will of God. Prayer was made continually for him. This seemed to detain him; but though grateful to his friends for their affection and sympathy, he felt almost that they were doing him a wrong. Any little alleviation of his symptoms was caught at by them, though not by himself. I saw him contending with mortal pain and weakness; and he intimated he would rather have his dismissal than be longer detained, and have to pass through again the conflict and suffering. He spoke—for his intellect was clear as his heart was calm—almost pathetically of his condition should he live— a helpless cripple, to linger out life, a burden to others, with a young and large family around him without means of support. So near to land, he naturally felt, and by Divine grace he felt, he did not wish to put to sea again. He felt the agony of dissolution, the wrenching of the taking down of the clay tabernacle; and, though unmurmuring and resigned, he would rather die. His prayer would be, as I gathered his sentiments and understood his feelings whilst sitting at his bedside, "Father, if it be Thy will, let this suffice."*

Here was the true man. Christianity is not asceticism. Affliction is not a luxury to be indulged in, or a price with which to purchase heaven. Nor is Christianity stoicism. Insensibility to suffering, whatever it may be, is not human. It is either above or below humanity. Shrinking from suffering is permissible; and we may lawfully, whilst submissively, pray for its alleviation, its shortening, and its end.

The approach of the enemy was sure, and there is no discharge in this war. How did our friend nerve himself for the conflict? and

* Appendix A.

how did he act in the fight? Come and see.
I myself was many times a witness; and
what I now state is the result of my own
observation,—what I saw with my own eyes,
and heard with my own ears, or what I
received from friends who were constantly
with him.

Death had approached him full armed,
with many weapons, and at many points of
attack; there was one in particular, over
which we must throw a veil. It was the
head, the stay, the husband, the father
upon whom the assault was made. But so
calm was our friend, the appearance of the
enemy produced no trepidation; so calm,
so well assured, his pulse did not quicken,
or add a unit to its beatings in the hottest
of the fight. Shall I tell you, friends,
what most impressed my eye and my
heart? In a grand historical picture there
must be some central object around
which all the rest culminate. It was so
here. Our friend lying gasping for breath,
one side paralysed, almost speechless, and
enduring mortal pain, presented to view the

Christian hero in the last and greatest battle driving the enemy before him, and covering him with shame and confusion. To my view I never before realized death so crest-fallen, humiliated, or shamed. Instead of the king of terrors brandishing his dart, he seemed despoiled of his arms, shorn of his strength, scared by the dying saint, and lost in confusion, fain to creep into any corner, or hide in any crevice, for fear of his own destruction. He appeared to my view cowed, faint-hearted, and lost. I speak the sentiments which impressed me at the time. I felt that I could hold him in contempt. The moral heroism and spiritual strength of our brother appeared in contrast. Oh how great! He was calm. It is only the greatly brave who are calm in battle.

We have referred to the soldier's prayer which was the immediate cause of Jasper's conversion. We admire heroism in the field of battle. It is a principle of our nature to admire what is sublime; and though grace will elevate and purify, it will never destroy what our Creator has given

us. There is something noble in the thought
of the soldier's going into battle calm in
spirit, intent on duty, and sustained by the
hope of victory. One of England's choicest
poets has well expressed the principle and
the fact :—

" Friend of the brave! in peril's darkest hour,
    Intrepid virtue looks to thee for power;
    To thee the heart its trembling homage yields,
    On stormy floods and carnage cover'd fields.
    When front to front the banner'd hosts combine,
    Halt ere they close, and form the dreadful line;
    When all is still on Death's devoted soil,
    The march-worn soldier mingles for the toil.
    As rings the glittering tube he lifts on high,
    The dauntless brow and spirit-speaking eye
    Hails in his heart the music yet to come,
    And hears thy stormy music in the drum."

Thus it is with the Christian warrior,
having for his helmet the hope of salvation.
The call to battle, the sound of alarm, the
shaking of the tabernacle, the whistling of
the winds through the dilapidated building,
—all this is music, the bugle call of angels
for the grand attack upon death's last
Redan.

When his brother, about the middle of his illness, anticipating the event, spoke to him relative to his experience and feelings in prospect of death, he said he had never had a doubt or fear : he sent his little boy for the Hymn-book, and said the two last verses of the hymn beginning, " Now I have found the ground wherein," expressed his experience—

" Though waves and storms go o'er my head,
    Though strength, and health, and friends be
      gone,—

When he came to the word friends, he exclaimed, bursting into tears, " Friends, friends, how many friends I have ! "

Though joys be wither'd all and dead,
    Though every comfort be withdrawn ;
On this my steadfast soul relies :
Father, thy mercy never dies.

" Fix'd on this ground will I remain,
    Though my heart fail, and flesh decay ;
This anchor shall my soul sustain,
    When earth's foundations melt away ;
Mercy's full power I then shall prove,
Loved with an everlasting love."

There was also another favourite hymn,

which he could never trust himself to use,
it so overpowered him :—

> "Thou Shepherd of Israel, and mine,
>   The joy and desire of my heart ;
> For closer communion I pine,
>   I long to reside where Thou art :
> The pasture I languish to find,
>   Where all who their Shepherd obey,
> Are fed, on Thy bosom reclined,
>   And screen'd from the heat of the day.

> "Ah ! show me that happiest place,
>   The place of Thy people's abode,
> Where saints in an ecstacy gaze,
>   And hang on a crucified God :
> Thy love for a sinner declare,
>   Thy passion and death on the tree ;
> My spirit to Calvary bear,
>   To suffer and triumph with Thee."

> "'T is there, with the lambs of Thy flock,
>   There only, I covet to rest,
> To lie at the foot of the rock,
>   Or rise to be hid in Thy breast ;
> 'Tis there I would always abide,
>   And never a moment depart ;
> Conceal'd in the cleft of Thy side,
>   Eternally held in Thy heart."

On one occasion, when his friends were
around his bed, speaking of his funeral,

referring to the Burial-Service, he requested
them—and he wished all his children and
near friends to be present—when it came to
that part where it is said, "We give Thee
hearty thanks for that it hath pleased Thee
to deliver this our brother out of the mis-
eries of this sinful world; beseeching Thee
that it may please Thee of Thy gracious
goodness shortly to accomplish the number
of Thine elect, and to hasten Thy kingdom."
—"When it comes to this part," he emphati-
cally said, "be sure all of you say Amen."
A kind friend, who, like a true sister of
mercy, was often with him, to render aid
in his sick and dying chamber, testifies that
she never saw the like patience at all times
exhibited under the extremest sufferings.
A murmur never escaped his lips; he was
entirely resigned to the Divine will; his
cheerful thankful spirit never forsook him;
and though he felt the anguish and that
mortal weakness, which none can imagine
unless they have witnessed it, or have in
some degree felt in their own persons what
it is, and under its influence wished to enter

into the haven of rest; yet did he, notwith-
standing, fully exemplify in his noble bear-
ing in these seasons of extremity the soul-
lifting words of the Apostle, " strengthened
with all might, according to His glorious
power, unto all patience and long-suffering
with joyfulness." He was more than con-
querer. His friends, whose very souls were
lacerated by the sight of his sufferings, will
hardly, now that they are all over, wish that
they had been less, since they thus wrought
out for him " a far more exceeding and eternal weight of glory."

I will only further say, in reference to
our brother's experience, he was habitually
and constantly happy; not that he was, as
we have seen, without his trials, but he did
not sink under them, but rose above them,
triumphing in Christ Jesus. St. Peter ex-
presses in a few words his Christian experience from first to last: " Unto you that
believe, Christ is precious:" " whom having
not seen, ye love; in whom, though now ye
see Him not, yet believing, ye rejoice with
joy unspeakable and full of glory."

And now we come to the final scene. The last noon on earth has arrived ; and ere to-morrow's dawn, on the ransomed spirit will open the light of heaven. He summoned his children around him : like Jacob waiting for his Lord's salvation, he gives them his dying counsel and prayers : triumphing in spirit, he would have them share his victory "Sing, children, sing!" the little ones obeyed, and faltered out, as well as they could, the pæan of victory. He then said, "*I have done with you now, children.*" Addressing those in the room, he said, "Jordan overflows his banks to-day : I'm right into the water. There is no ferry boat to take me over. 'Ignorance' found a boatman at the place, one 'Vain-Hope,' and got him to ferry him over ; but that would not do. You thought (addressing his brother) some time ago that I was dying, but I did not ; now I feel that I am. I am right in the water to the bottom. I feel as though I was walking and talking with God. I see Christ standing at the beautiful gate, and the shining ones all around Him. Hark! do

you not hear the music?" They said they
could not. "Bend down; put your ear close
to mine; I never heard anything like it."
Oh, no! it was no delusion,—no play of
the fancy,—no delirium of the fevered brain.
There *was* music there, the song of angels,
the everlasting chimes, the play of God's
free, bounteous spirit, the bliss of Paradise,
the joy of the Redeemed. The soul was
attuned to heavenly melody; the swell of
the organ of the blest, the sweet cadences
of the Golden Harp, distant music from
the spirit-land struck the ear of the dying
man. Soberly, I say, this was no hallu-
cination. Did not Nebuchadnezzar see four
walking in the burning fiery furnace, and
the form of the fourth was like the Son of
God: his courtiers and attendants did not
see this glorious form, but Nebuchadnezzar
himself did. In the dreadful agony of our
Lord, an angel was sent from heaven to
strengthen Him. Did Peter and James and
John, though present in the garden, see the
angel? I think not. But Jesus did. Paul
was caught up into paradise, and heard

unspeakable words, but whether in the body
or out of the body he could not tell. No
other mortal man saw those sights or heard
those words; but Paul did. It was fact, not
fancy; and no doubt it was thus at the
bedside of our departed friend. As, in
answer to prayer, the Lord opened the eyes
of the prophet's servant to see the mountain
full of horses and chariots of fire round
about Elisha, so he saw forms bright and
luminous, and heard music sweet and melo-
dious, which dear friends close to him could
neither see nor hear. He wished those now
in the room to sing; but this was impossible.
"Ah! your harp, I see, is on the willows:
I am close to Jerusalem." He urged his
beloved partner, who with untiring assiduity*
watched over him through all his illness, to
say, in the language of the hymn,—

> "Oh! should'st Thou call me to resign
> What most I prize; it ne'er was mine,
> I only yield Thee what was Thine,
>   Thy will be done."

After this he lay silent and motionless;

* Appendix C.

occasionally, however, he would attempt to raise his arm, and would say, " More than conqueror,—more than conqueror." He lay quite silent: when about nine o'clock, he inquired,—showing his distinct recollection and clearness of intellect,—" Who preached at chapel this evening ? I suppose they preached Christ." The Saviour's precious name, the anointed one, the Father's elect and beloved one, the Son of God, the only name in which is salvation, was the last word on his lips upon earth; and ere the sound had well-nigh died away his sanctified spirit was free, and his sufferings over for ever: partner of the sufferings of Christ, he was thenceforth to be the partner of His glory

This triumph in death is not peculiar to Methodism; but it has been truly remarked, that Methodists die well. This circumstance has attracted the attention of ministers and people of other communions. What shall we say to this ? We claim no special privilege, yet we think we can offer some explanation. We give prominence to the doctrine of conversion; the cross is kept always in view; experience of a death unto sin and a new birth unto righteousness is insisted on; and the testimony of God's Spirit to our spirits that we are the children of God. We preach repentance, a conscious pardon, a realized holiness and meetness for heaven; therefore when the true Methodist comes to die, he has not to cast about him for evidences, or to seek a preparation, but he is ready; he has "oil in his vessel with his lamp." This a thousand death-beds have testified, and hence the triumphant language of our hymns; and thus the desire of many, when death is drawing near to them, they would like to see a Methodist.

And now, dear friends, what is the lesson we are to learn from the teaching of such a life and such a death? not of one from a distance, of another nation or of another age, but of one of yourselves,—one who has lived all his life among you, whom you all know?

There are three things it teaches me: first, the power of religion; secondly, the nature of religion; and thirdly the common-

ness of religion. God grant it may teach
these lessons to us all.

I. The power of religion. What is power?
It is an attribute of God. Power is sublime.
Oh, what power is there in the pyramids,
in the steam-engine, in modern artillery!
Then, again, what power is there in mind,
whether of science or of art! what marvel-
lous power to move is put on canvas, and
wrought in marble! what sublime power is
it to paint by the sunbeam; to converse over
seas and continents by lightning; to bring
the invisible into sight, and ascend the
heights of space, and look into the stars!
But all this range of power dwindles into
insignificance before the omnipotence of God;
it is all dwarfed by the power of religion.
The Gospel of Jesus did more for Jasper
Stickland than all the philosophers com-
bined together in all ages have ever done in
elevating the moral and spiritual condition
of man. I defy the whole world of infidels
and unbelievers of every shape and colour
to produce such a trophy as has been dis-
played to your view to-night. The power of

God on Jasper dwarfs all the most triumphant achievements of man.

II. It teaches us the nature of religion.
With Paul, we preach Christ crucified;
with him also we say, "Christ is risen;"
with him we teach, "If we have been
planted in the likeness of His death, we
shall be also in the likeness of His resur-
rection." Christ crucified only, is but half
the Gospel. It must be Christ alive again
to constitute the whole Gospel. Now, then,
upon this theory, or rather upon this Scrip-
ture truth, where must Christ now be?
Where? Surely, if anywhere, in the hearts
of His members. If He died for them,—
and they, in effect and by law, died in Him,
—surely if He is raised again, and if they
have risen in Him, He must live in them.
"Christ," says St. Paul, "that liveth in me."
This, then, is the nature of religion, or
Christianity. It is conversion and salvation;
it is a new nature,—the putting off the old
man, and the putting on the new. It is
exchanging darkness for light, a guilty con-
science for conscious pardon and acceptance

with God, misery for happiness, the world for God, hell for heaven. This is the Gospel-religion; and whatever does not reach to this, or is inconsistent with it, I will not acknowledge to be religion in the Gospel sense. Where I find this religion, I will acknowledge as a friend and a brother one who is thus with Christ and for God. He may be found among Papists and among Puseyites, amongst religionists of various names; his creed may be very defective, his views of religion in many things very erroneous; but if he has Christ, whatever he may have besides, or whatever else he lacks, I will gladly own him as a brother beloved, as my brother. We often err; we fail in the charity of our Redeemer. He is meek and lowly; a bruised reed He will not break, and the smoking flax He will not quench. In our zeal for orthodoxy, we crucify charity: it often savours more of Jehu than of Jesus. On the other hand, what shall I say of those whose only religion is form; whose only baptism is water; whose only sacrament is bread and wine, and not the Lord's body ; whose confession to man is a substitute for contrition for sin and confession to God ; who are content with a fellow-creature's absolution, and have never heard the voice of Jesus in their hearts ; who seem to think the priest stands in the same relation to the soul as the physician does to the body, having the form, but denying the power of godliness. We see in our late friend Jaspar the nature and character of true religion ; and we would say to all professors, produce us such examples as this, and we will acknowledge you.

III. The third lesson we are taught by the example before us is the commonness of true religion. Say what you will, it is designed for the common people. Say what you will, it is very common ; for it is designed for all men, and therefore styled, the " common salvation." It is not confined to any rank ; it lays hold of a few mighty and noble, as well as of many humble and poor. It is lofty enough for the grandest palace ; it is lowly enough for the meanest hovel. It is welcome to the happiest and most joyous circles; it can kill the fatted calf and be merry; and it can cheer the gloomiest dungeon, and sing the songs of Zion, and shout the praises of Jesus in a prison. Oh! it is *very* common; it gauges all intellects, and acts equally on all; it blends in unison and fellowship the feeblest and the most powerful of minds. It is so common, we cannot tell to which sex it most properly belongs, or which it most adorns. It is equally beautiful in every period of life. Oh! the harmonius concert, when young men and maidens, old men and children, together praise the Lord. These precious moral diamonds are not rare: they are in your towns, villages, hamlets, houses, shops, and fields. They are beacons, to warn the voyagers of shoals and quicksands; they are direction-posts, to show the way to the City of Refuge; watchmen on the walls of Zion, who cry day and night; heralds of salvation, proclaiming the grace of Christ; they are lepers who have washed in the fountain and have been made clean, and they invite you to the same healing; they have quenched their thirst at the river of the water of life, and they invite you to come and drink. Examples like that of our friend are not rare examples. We say, indeed, he was a Christian man of singular excellence; but we do not mean by this to disparage the worth of others, or to say such excellence is unfrequent. You see in a grand gallery a beautiful painting; it strikes you very much, and you say, "Oh, look at this!" but a stolid ignorance alone would suppose that you thought no other picture worth looking at. Christ's precious ones: every jewel in His diadem is excellent, though some may have more lustre than others; every one is excellent, even that one that emits the feeblest light, and is most obscured for want of polish. I say every one of them is seen by the Father, though you may not see them; and recognised by Him, though you may disown them. Compared with the world, it is a little flock; but, as witnesses for God, they are a cloud of witnesses. The gate through which they enter is strait, and the way in which they

walk is narrow, when compared with the
wide gate and the broad way, but still, they
are a company which no man can number,
out of every kingdom and people. This
religion is common, not one of you but may
get it. All of you look at it in this glass I
have set before you, and let the infidel
acknowledge that he sees a *man*.

Infidelity shrivels and blasts man's powers,
cramps his intellect, spreads mildew on
his feelings, lays its icy hand upon his heart,
and blows out his soul, as it would the light
of a taper. I say to the infidel, "here is a
man to equal whom you will search in vain
in all your ranks, which your principles
never have produced, and which they never
will or can produce." You know that this
testimony is true. Your own discomfort
misgivings, and unrest prove it: quitting
the ark, like Noah's raven, you return to and
fro, and do not, like the dove, seek to be
taken in again. Yet the waters do not re-
cede, and land is no nearer in view. Miser-
able men, who attempt to do without God!
Your own school confesses its wretchedness,

and the superior claims of the Gospel. Rousseau was struck with, and acknowledged, the contrast. " In Christ," says he, " we have an example of a quiet and peaceable spirit, of a becoming modesty, and sobriety; just and honest, upright and sincere ; and, above all, of a most gracious and benevolent temper and behaviour. One who did no wrong, no injury to any man; in whose mouth was no guile ; who went about doing good, not only by His preaching and ministry, but also in curing all manner of diseases among the people. His life was a beautiful picture of human nature, when in its native simplicity and purity ; and showed at once what excellent creatures men would be, when under the influence and power of that Gospel which He preached to them. I confess that the majesty of the Scriptures and the holiness of the Gospel greatly affect me. View the books of the philosophers, with all their pomp; how little do they appear placed beside this ! Is it possible that a book at once so sublime and simple can be the work of men? Does He speak in the tone of an

enthusiast, or of an ambitious sectary ? What
mildness, what purity in His manners! What
persuasive grace in His instructions! What
elevation in His maxims! What profound
wisdom in His discourses! What presence
of mind, what ingenuity, and what justness
in His answers! What empire over His
passions! Where is the man, where is the
sage, who knows how to act, to suffer, and
to die, without weakness and without osten-
tation ? " This is the testimony, the remarkable testimony of an infidel. Will the friends
of Jesus endorse this testimony ? Say, you
lovers of your Saviour, is Jesus worthy of
this praise ? He is worthy; and the life and
death of Jasper Stickland is a justification,
an illustration, and a confirmation of this
praise.

To the formalist I would say, "here is a
man who has religion, the genuine thing;
why do you parody it ? God will blast you
and your forms together if you have not,
and are content to do without, the Spirit of
Christ. You have the form of a Christ,—a
dead Christ,—a mere image or idol ; no

more vitality in him than in a heathen god: the spark of life has not yet been struck into your soul." To the hypocrite I would say, " As our dear departed friend honoured the Gospel, you disgrace it. Imperfect Christian, you may be saved, but as it were by fire, and your work will suffer loss. You have had a perfect Christian exhibited before you this evening, and you see the blessedness of the work of grace fully carried out. Feeble and timid one, be not discouraged ; let no distance between your experience and his discourage you. " *Cheer up*," our dear friend would say to the feeblest of you: "Cheer up; try, try again." Be not discouraged ; look with gladness upon the smallest spark of grace, and let that little glimmering of light kindle to a flame ; kindle it at the cross ; take it to Christ, and get Christ to light it in your hearts ; and then, with our departed friend, you, the feeblest of Christ's followers, will become a bright and shining light.

I might draw many more useful lessons, and bring under review many other persons, but time fails. Surely enough has been said, both for conviction and for encouragement. The reasons for embracing Christianity, this heart religion we have contemplated, are endless; the motives, one would think, are overwhelming. Surely "godliness is profitable unto all things, having promise of the life that now is, and of that which is to come." To sum up the matter, as it regards the believer, let the great Apostle express it: "For all things are yours, whether Paul, or Apollos, or Cephas, or the world, or life, or death, or things present, or things to come; all are yours, and ye are Christ's, and Christ is God's." The true foundation of our text is this, ye are " heirs of God and joint heirs with Christ." And thus the whole verse reads: "And if children, then heirs; heirs of God, and joint heirs with Christ; if so be that we suffer with Him, that we may be also glorified together." It is not heaven that God gives us; it is not grace merely that God gives us; it is not, so to speak, even glory: but it is something higher, and greater, and more everlasting than even grace or glory,—God gives you

Christ; God gives you Himself; God is your own God. That is the portion of God's people. The Gospel tells them so; the Gospel gives them the right, and puts them into possession.

Dear friends—all who now hear me—let me entreat that this bright example be not lost. See what grace can do. Delay not; yield to the charm; fall beneath its power. "And they shall be Mine, saith the Lord of Hosts, in that day when I make up My jewels; and I will spare them, as a man spareth his own son that serveth him."

—oo°o°oo—

APPENDIX A.

THIS fellowship with Christ's sufferings is beautifully described by Keble ;—that bursting forth at times of anguish, that dissolving weakness—all my bones are out of joint—that distressing cry for help ; and yet, amidst it all, profound submission to the will of God, no murmur, no complaint.

> "Thou who did'st sit on Jacob's well
>   The weary hour of noon ;
> The languid pulses Thou can'st tell,
>   The nerveless spirit tune.
> Thou from whoso cross in anguish burst
> The cry that own'd Thy dying thirst,
> To Thee we turn, our last and first,
>   Our sun and soothing moon."

Again,—

> "On the tedious cross
> Told the long hours of death, as, ono by ono,
> The life-strings of that tender heart gave way ;
>   Even sinners taught by Thee
>   Look sorrow in tho face,
> And bid her froely welcomo,   "

And once more,—

> "Thus everywhere we find our suffering God,
>   And where He trod
> May set our steps: the Cross on Calvary
>   Uplifted high
> Beams on the martyr host, a beacon light
>   In open fight.
>
> To the still wrestlings of the lonely heart
>   He doth impart
> The virtue of His midnight agony,
>   When none was nigh,
> Save God and one good angel, to assuage
>   The tempest's rage."

A clergyman filling high official position, whose duties gave him opportunities of extensive observation both at home and abroad, informed me that he had found the Methodists very partial to Keble. There can be no doubt of the fact. It would be strange were it not so, since almost every Methodist regards his Hymn-book, as the devout Churchman does the Liturgy, as embodying all his wants and wishes,—placing the most appropriate words in his mouth to offer unto God. Now Keble's poetry is in perfect accord with Wesley's. There is the same impression of sinfulness and weakness; the

same dependence on Christ, and glorying
alone in Him. The affections centre in the
cross; the soul breathes after holiness; and
there is the same abandonment of the whole
heart to God. The language of Wesley is
much more abrupt; the glare of the eternal
world more awful; the thunder rolls more
grandly; and the lightning flashes more
vividly. Wesley's deals but little with figure,
and there is scarce any play of fancy in his
compositions. Keble is softer and more re-
fined: his pages are more adapted to a
cultivation which did not usually obtain in
Wesley's day. But there is equal intense-
ness of feeling, and an equal amount of
power; and, blessed be God, the influence
of both Keble and Wesley is spreading all
over the world, and increasing more and
more. By them God has made rich provision for His saints; and in their words will
His people offer up their heart-felt sacrifices,
and at their shrines will they kindle their
devotion, from age to age, until the consum-
mation of all things.

As a specimen from each of these gifted

and sainted men of that "boundless charity divine" which forms, as it were, the staple of Methodism, I add the following lines, exhibiting both parallel and contrast, and forming together a grand harmony :—

Wesley—

"Ontcasts of men, to yon I call,
    Harlots, and publicans, and thieves!

"Come, O my guilty brethren, come,
    Groaning beneath your load of sin ;
His bleeding heart shall make yon room ;
    His open side shall take you in."

Keble—

"Nor can ye not delight to think
    Where He vonchsafed to eat,
How the Most Holy did not shrink
    From tonch of sinners meat;
What worldly hearts, and hearts impure,
    Went with Him throngh the rich man's door,
That we might learn of Him lost souls to love,
And view His least and worst with hope to
    meet above."

I am tempted to refer to two other compositions of equal power and beauty. It will be seen that the style and treatment are as dissimilar as the principle and spirit of them are alike.

Wesley—

> " Turn the full stream of nature's tide ;
>   Let all our actions tend
> To Thee their Source ; Thy love the guide,
>   Thy glory be the end.

> " Earth then a scale to heaven shall be ;
>   Sense shall point out the road ;
> The creatures all shall lead to Thee,
>   And all we taste be God."

Keble—

> " Thenceforth, to eyes of high desire,
>   The meanest things below,
> As with a seraph's robe of fire
>   Invested, burn and glow :

> " The rod of Heaven has touch'd them all,
>   The word from Heaven is spoken ;
> ' Rise, shine, and sing, thou captive thrall :
>   ' Are not thy fetters broken ?

> ' The God who hallow'd thee and blest
>   ' Pronouncing thee all good—
> ' Hath He not all thy wrongs redrest,
>   ' And all thy bliss renew'd ?' "

APPENDIX B.

---◦◦◦---

AN ACCOUNT OF THE FUNERAL OF JASPER STICKLAND.

On Monday, June 10th, 1867, the mortal remains of this deeply regretted servant of Christ, who had been called away in the midst of his days and of his usefulness, were consigned to the silent chambers of the grave.

About three or four hundred persons were present at the funeral, so that the church was full while the first part of the service was read; and a numerous throng surrounded the grave, and listened in solemn silence to the language of hope and confidence, which might so unhesitatingly be employed with reference to "the soul of their dear brother departed."

As he had belonged to The Foresters' Friendly Society, many of its members attended, to show their respect for the deceased; and one of them, before they quitted the churchyard, read a paper, in which the expression of resignation to the will of the Great Disposer of events was associated with the utterance of regret for the loss of a friend and brother.

His favourite hymn—beginning,

" Jesus wept! those tears are over,
But his heart is still the same :"—

was sung upon the occasion with deep and genuine feeling. The closing lines in the last verse,—

" Thou art all in all to me,
Loving One of Bethany,"—

had been a great comfort to him upon his dying bed.

Conspicuous in the long line of mourners was a little company of children, who, as they followed the lifeless body of their beloved father to the cold, dark grave, were weeping and sobbing as if their hearts would break.

It was a sight enough to melt a heart of

stone ; and many a manly breast there heaved with sympathetic feeling.

It is to be hoped that the sympathy which has been called forth will assume a practical form, for the benefit of the widow and her large family of fatherless children, since it is written, Let us not love in word only, but in deed and in truth.

EDWARD FISON.

APPENDIX C.

———◦◦———

I WILL relate one circumstance which will shew the watchful care taken of this sainted sufferer. His wife and her sister who was living with them watched constantly at his bedside, or relieved one another in this affectionate service. His medical attendant was not a religious man, nor remarkable for soft expressions in his visits to the sick poor. Perhaps somewhat otherwise, as the sequel will tend to show. Mr. —— attended at this bedside with the most exemplary fidelity, and bestowed all the care and attention to the case which he could have given to his most wealthy patient. No doubt his perspicacity discovered sterling worth of character—the true man—amidst his lowly and humble surroundings. He likewise admired the exemplary behaviour manifested in the sick room, the care taken of his

patient, and the way in which his instructions were carried out. One day Mr. ——,
who is able to speak with authority, in a
tone of command said to the wife and
sister-in-law, "Follow me." He went down
stairs, led them out to his carriage, which
was waiting at the door, and said to his
servant, "Do you see these two women?"
"Yes, sir." "They are two then that I have
never blown up." The servant replied,
"Then, master, they *must* *be* something
remarkable."

————∞∘⊱⊰∘c∘————

APPENDIX D.

WHATEVER tends to throw light on character, or to illustrate the dealings of God with
His people, is interesting and profitable. A
circumstance or two which I omitted to mention I may here supply. There was about
Jasper Stickland a beautiful simplicity and
naturalness of character. There was nothing
strained, nothing put on, no cant, nothing
said without full and proper conception of
its meaning, nothing of the parrot kind in
his utterances. He was an Israelite indeed,
in whom there was no guile. With reference
to the verse,

> " Jesus can make a dying bed
> Feel soft as downy pillows are,"

he said his bed was not one of down. Again,
in the lines,

> " Labour is rest, and pain is sweet,
> If Thou my God, art here,"

he dropped the poetry in the fact, and said he did not find it so. With his perfect resignation and cheerful acquiescence in all the will of God, he still felt trial to be trial, suffering to be suffering, and weariness something different from repose. More than conqueror he was truly; but then the fight tested all his strength.

> " 'Tis so in war—the champion true
> Loves victory more, when dim in view
> He sees her glories gild afar
> The dusky edge of stubborn war,
> Than if the untrodden bloodless field
> The harvest of her laurels yield;
> Let not my bark in calm abide,
> But win her fearless way against the chafing tide."

This aptness and sincerity—the spirit and genuineness of the little child—is expressed in his photograph. (*See Frontispiece.*)

Another circumstance I would mention, and leave every one to form his own opinion of the statement, and make what inferences from it he likes. In the course of his illness, I called on him several times, but did not converse much with him, and never once asked him to join in prayer. I saw what he had to contend with from pain and weakness, and that every effort was painful. I could feel also that the Divine Spirit was supporting him—the unction of the Holy One—so that he needed little help from man. I knew how he loved his wife and children, and as I had formed the purpose, or rather God had put it into my heart, that they should never want after his removal, I many times thought of telling him he need not be careful or troubled about this matter, for I would befriend them. But I never once intimated to him what my intention was in this respect. I saw his Abrahamic faith, and it appeared to me almost impertinence to assure him that his dear family should have my support and interest, when he had so entirely placed them in the hands of a loving and covenant-keeping God.

I will also say—and I am fully aware of the evil of exaggeration, and therefore would most carefully avoid the slightest approach to it, and in such a beautiful character as this anything of the kind would sadly mar its fine and just proportions, yet I feel constrained to say—that he approached very nearly to perfection; and that I never witnessed in him any failing or any fault, and I never saw anything in him that I could wish to be otherwise. No doubt but that he felt his own weakness and sinfulness; and that as he was highly esteemed by his dear friends and all who knew him, the feelings that possessed his heart were those to which expression is given in the Prophet— "Then shalt thou remember and be confounded, and no more open thy mouth for the shame when I am pacified toward thee for all that thou hast done."

www.ingramcontent.com/pod-product-compliance
Lightning Source LLC
Chambersburg PA
CBHW020239090426
42735CB00010B/1762